It's 3am in Santa Cruz

Terrance Millet

Published by Terrance Millet, 2023.

While every precaution has been taken in the preparation of this book, the publisher assumes no responsibility for errors or omissions, or for damages resulting from the use of the information contained herein.

IT'S 3AM IN SANTA CRUZ

First edition. July 11, 2023.

Copyright © 2023 Terrance Millet.

ISBN: 979-8215818770

Written by Terrance Millet.

Table of Contents

It's 3AM in Santa Cruz
Terrance Lane Millet

For Denise

IN TIME OF DAFFODILS
in time of daffodils (who know
the goal of living is to grow)
forgetting why, remember how
in time of lilacs who proclaim
the aim of waking is to dream,
remember so (forgetting seem)
in time of roses (who amaze
our now and here with paradise)
forgetting if, remember yes
in time of all sweet things beyond
whatever mind may comprehend,
remember seek (forgetting find)
and in mystery to be
(when time from time shall set us free)
forgetting me, remember me
- e.e. cummings

Thanks to Tracy Daugherty for looking over this manuscript and making much-needed suggestions; to David Turkel for reading early drafts of some of these poems; to my wife Denise for her patience and proof-reading; to Karelia Stetz-Waters for her appreciation and for sharing some of these poems with her family; to Frieda Sherman for her friendship and support while we wrote and slammed poetry in the city; and to Santa Cruz as it was in its incarnation before the Loma Prieta earthquake—and the people who belonged to it.

How Faintly Call The Buoys

You've made your pilgrimage
    to Rome dropped hours of your life
    into a hand no longer Caesar's and how
    subtle were the trees along the avenue how
    quietly they leaved and caught the wind
    the mists are thinning and little
    islands take their places in the sun now
    eyes of herons look upon the waters of your years
    beneath these clouds (whose high and purple bellies in
    the morning now are brighter than your eyes can bear) the
    terns fly higher than the rising sun their
    flight is bright as lightning is
    like light above this quiet lake how
    clearly call the buoys it is the language
    of the light that calls through
    clearing fogs in winds and trees in
    leaves it is
    the reaching and soft heaving of the sun it
    is another spring

Rooftop

~ for Mother 1944

High on a roof a woman is knitting she
is gravid and the rooftop is flat tarred
and covered with pebbles she
sits on a folding chair making small
woollen booties beside her a
baby's cap is folded on a towel she
is careful with her work and
her needles move fast and sure they
click with regularity and
never cease their rhythm even
when she lifts her gaze to pop-
corn clouds racing overhead big-
bellied with beginnings

The Operator's Daughter

~ for Cheryl Millet 1947-2019

Sometimes a moment opens in her mind and
she is little when winter comes her
father puts storm windows up where summer screens
once were at the bottom of the frame a
wooden flap seals off three ventilation holes
in the morning she pushes up the sash
and lifts the flap to press her nose
against the holes and breathe
cold winter air that smells (she
knows) of ozone she
holds her hands up to
the patterns of thick frost upon the glass
and melts small handprints there then scrapes
frost off with fingernails to
place upon her tongue and
taste the winter melting in her mouth

One Summer Day

Upstream past memory and rapids
   old shadows move they
   are the dreams of my father he
   looks up suddenly happy and casts a lure
   far out upon the river soon he
   will take the train to Timmins and
   meet my mother "Twiz," he calls her he
   will bring her back to their first house but
   now the day is still the wind is quiet
   he stands upon the rocky bank
   his pipe smoke curling in the air
   his feet at ease inside the current's tug

Viewshed

Soft blades of light carve this church's gloom
   red and yellow columns of it lean
   across the pews they
   cling to icons by the empty organ pipes
   — outside leaves rustle in a wind that's
   rushing from the stones rolling the dead into the loam
   grinding the white fever of my father's bones
   into my own

The World of Waking Reality

(Borges: "I was talking with...who, in the world of waking reality, died many
years ago..."

A writer pictures a world
    in which all works are thought to be
    the creation of one author who
    is atemporal and anonymous plagiarism
    does not exist there and critics invent authors
    they "select two dissimilar works"—the Tao Te Ching
    and 1001 Nights, say—attribute them
    to the same writer and then "determine
    most scrupulously
    the psychology of this interesting author."
    tonight I am trying
    to wrap my understanding around this it
    is as though an alien were to consider all art
    and literature to be the product of a single
    planetary organism — humanity — and
    the psychology of that single organism
    is the simultaneous compilation of all the human beings
    who have ever lived or will live
    tugging
    at my attention is the notion
    that a significant insight waits along the pathway of this inquiry
    meanwhile in Portland a naked woman
    confronts a line of armed police she
    sits lotus-like on the intersection they have cordoned off
    they avert their stares they
    enter their cars and drive away
    seen in light of the paradigm above

it is as though a leucocyte confronts a cluster
of invasive cancer cells healing
a small area on the body of humanity
something pulls at me somewhere
in Borge's mind are the words
"a book that does not contain its counterbook
is considered
incomplete"

Portrait

In a house on a hill a woman
    leans against a counter
    surrounded by men whose wits
    are rapiers she walks
    through rooms furnished with re-
    cumbancies of living and out
    to the lawn's lip where grass
    falls greenly away her dog
    runs to the point where the earth
    meets the sky it
    resembles a wolf wild
    and shaggy her
    lovers follow calling "Come back"
    but the animal turns to the woman it
    stops at her feet she
    looks into its eyes and feels
    a sudden link with its wildness something
    outside her humanity
    she's charged with
    possibilities too large for the space
    around her
    faraway the voices of men
    lament they shape the air with her name
    but she wears the wind and the sky
    (mirrored on the lens of her eyes) is a pond
    where shimmering clouds race

It's 3am in Santa Cruz

He gazes at the title of books moves
    a touch over covers tentative as though
    some message in braille lay hidden
    it's 3 am in Santa Cruz and
    he's still married to the land to
    the perspective that was
    Greece he's lost —he can't say what—
    for leaving but feels it then comes across
    a note from Ben Jonson--"The ravens sat all
    night beating the air
    with their obstreperous beaks"

Storms

At times a turmoil in a dream
    disturbs us and a figure
    in the distance battling the wind calls
    us away to new places ...perhaps
    camping on a hilltop naked in a storm
    and finding someone half-frozen comatose we
    bring them into the tent amazed at our discovery and
    hold them skin to skin knowing this
    to be the only way to quicken buried lives letting
    the warmth rise we pull their hypothermic form
    close it begins to stir eyelids opening
    over a bottomless gaze
    such
    nights are restless thawing
    out our animas bringing
    ourselves back to life and
    with a little luck we may
    yet be free inside the storm may
    dance clothesless in the wind burning
    with our own heat what
    this means while we're sitting at our daily
    bread is not clear when it's overcast when
    newspapers litter the room when
    life unwinds its idleness in the air when
    we have stir-fry for supper and buy
    the groceries on the way home
    nothing seems changed in daylight re-
    membrance of the wind's tug on our skin of
    the rain tapping with a temperature that was our own
    thins like mist on a pond but

the memory of those impossible new eyes
opening into ours
does not pass away so easily and
our feet tighten beneath the table as though sprung
with some new need to dance

On the Beach With Carl Jung

A man with white hair
    points over the sea to an evening's
    bright stars and
    explains the universe
    his utterance
    is an image of word shapes
    around lacunae from which
    a sentence has fallen into my mind
    "we must when trying to understand creation
    see all things as metaphors and know
    the divinity as a distant ocean whose influence
    upon us is the equivalent
    of tides and gravities..."
    to bring such knowing
    to this side of dreaming Jung writes
    that the developed self is a blend
    of opposing truths he
    calls it coincidentia oppositorium
    —coinciding opposites
    Carl Jung is on a beach I do not understand
    where an old man's words
    reveal all objects in the universe
    to be metaphors of meaning
    —to see them whole is to understand
    existence— wherein the shadows
    of our alphabet are dreams as
    old as memory
    new as desire
    they murmur that all objects are divine
    and have two meanings

one manifest one hidden
Kazantzakis says the doors
to here and there are adjacent and
identical . . . . both green
both beautiful

The Aleph

A woman notices that
    what she thought to be a freckle
    is in fact a small mole diminutive and nascent
    perching
    on the inner mound of her right breast
    and with a little shock she realizes
    there is such a one identically located on her mother
    and on her aunt she
    wonders with sudden urgency
    if it is on her grandmother's breast as well
    and yes she remembers yes
    it has a sudden and unexpected history
    she has no way of knowing how extensive
    that history is or who in the long line of women
    had it first she feels an overwhelming
    tenderness toward this link to generations of women
    now freshly present on her a link unutterably
    feminine and she imagines the moles small delicate
    identically placed to be the object of countless
    husbands' love each foolish man thinking
    it was uniquely his to covet to cherish but
    each was one of many a multitude of marks
    stretching back in time stretch-
    ing forward linking the women like waves
    of an ocean that individual men
    merely drift upon she
    does not know precisely
    what to do with this notion with
    the deeps beneath those waves but
    she is aware the mole had flowered hiding itself

as an irrelevancy and she
never registered its genealogy
until tonight the diminutive bloom might
in and of itself contain a huge
significance what might such things mean and
would it be dangerous
for her future husband as a male to become
conscious
of these links in an unbroken chain
she pursues her thoughts the
discovery makes her feel close to the women
of her family the quiditatis or "whatness"
of the family female beyond time
in each of them the young woman
her mother her aunt her grandmother
as though she glimpses a portion of a great
mystery that they are a part of ––conscious
nodes of female power channeled
by the cosmos through them and
she wonders ––how many other such mysteries exist
seen but never noticed con-
necting women together in the great
immortal and inconceivably feminine?
Borges writes that "The Faithful
who gather at the mosque of Amr, in Cairo
are acquainted with the fact that the entire universe
lies inside one of the stone pillars that ring its central court
... No one, of course, can actually see it, but those
who lay an ear against the surface tell that
after some short while
they perceive its busy hum..."

For Elin

~ and Karelia
    In quiet rooms their fingers
    linger over letters in the books
    they love
    their messages declare
    how love and life
    achieve a presence in a world be-
    yond the men and women
    who are midwives to their metaphors...
    Borges writes that certain truths attempt
    to join us in reality he writes of Kubla Khan
    and Xanadu emerging from a dream
    into a poem by an Englishman...
    meantime the air moves faintly
    over ferns and yellow daffodils
    across
    new leaves upon japonica it
    tugs a wooden wind chime's cupped
    clapper (gently blowing) in
    these small movements
    old memories breathe they
    separate particulars of motion they
    ride the lily's fragrant moment they
    carry us to waters
    where our dreams come down to drink

Peggy

A man wrenched from sleep
    by a woman shrieking beneath his window
    cannot place the voice or where he is then
    the accent brings it home he is on leave
    and it is 1973 in Santa Cruz "Daddy!" she cries
    "It's me, Peggy I
    love you, Daddy Ohh I killed him"
    "Stop Stop that!" a male voice pleads
    the man in the window looks down
    a woman hunched in the street
    confronts a man "I did"
    says the woman "I killed him he
    was the kindest man he worked so hard
    doing all the menial things to help people
    and when he was sick nobody
    would pay for his hospital bills nobody
    would help him after all he did for other people
    I love you Daddy I helped you no one else would"
    "Stop talking like that" says the man in the street
    "He was suffering and sick and no one would help him
    so I helped him I killed him and
    now I want to be with him I want to go where he is"
    "Oh God please stop"
    "Daddy, it's Peggy It's Peggy"
    the woman is drunk
    she delivers this confession in a clear, high voice
    her arms wrapped round an old steel lamp post
    the man in the window shudders
    he looks at his watch it is three a.m.
    the hour of long and lonely damnations of

mortality a daughter
helping her father die a man
deserted another war a woman
calling in the night
"It's me. It's me, Peggy"

Bloemen Velden

~ for Miesje Van Tol

23

At Keukenhof the hyacinth are
    purple streams between the banks of tulips
    they flow between trees bordered
    by green grasses they
    lead to ponds she
    skips among the waters where the sun
    comes down to drink a sun
    that's high and young upon her head
    and face she wakes among these flowers she
    walks and sleeps among them now
    the gardens in a young girl's mind
    that rooted there and bloomed and
    never left

Somewhere in Time

Somewhere in time a Jesuit is writing
    that Gerard Manley Hopkins fails God
    because he writes poetry

    in Greece[1] Nikos Kazantzakis is writing
    the doors to heaven and to hell are equal and adjacent
    both green both beautiful
    and is excommunicated
    in America Peter Matthieson is writing a calamity
    about priests, missions, and first people he
    is titling it
    <u>At Play in the Fields of the Lord</u>
    in Rome, the secret archives are claiming
    that Jesus has red hair
    like David before him that
    he is long-legged and walking quickly
    somewhere in time
    he is sitting by a camp fire
    on a Galilee beach listening to the stories
    of men and women as they eat fish
    and grainy bread he
    throws his head back he
    is laughing
    some things are hidden in the arithmetics
    of faith while on the tomb of Kazantzakis
    (which crowns a hilltop looking down
    upon the church that banished him)
    these words appear: *I hope for nothing*

    I fear nothing I am free[2]

A Parable

A young man's mother once lived in a tree be-
    fore her children were born she
    wore her hair long her dresses home-made
    and her feet bare she
    believed in love and practiced it
    in a world that was wide & good but
    in her mind the world grew to be a dangerous place
    from which she sought to protect her children she
    left the tree and moved into a house
    became strict from duty and from new love she
    taught her children to be wary of free-thinkers of heresy
    she took them to church and read the Bible
    one day the young man asked his mother
    why her Jesus slept under the trees of Nazareth why
    he sat beneath them barefoot and preached love and
    acceptance under their boughs he
    asked why the critics of her saviour accused the
    Nazarene of being a free-thinker and a heretic and
    wasn't it ironic (the young man asked) that
    from the living trees under which he taught
    a cross was made and
    it was upon the dead tree that the man died
    what
    was the meaning of it all the young man asked had
    his mother been a hippie and
    why did she move out of a tree and into a house
    made from trees that were dead
    the
    young man's mother had no answer but
    her mind was troubled a truth

long buried and forgotten began to sprout
over the years it spread its branches
through her mind and these branches she
considered to be her thoughts when her children
were grown the mother left the church and
her husband and
moved to a cottage in the woods where she
wandered among the trees and
as she walked she sang
What
did the mother sing?
The young
man had become a composer who
created music filled with the sound
of winds he
brought the wood in the instruments back to life
and the music they made were the songs
his mother sang as she walked beneath
the boughs of the living trees

Her Woman's Heart

In one of time's moments
	a child on a beach watches her father
	dive into the waves and disappear
	minutes pass and
	the child begins to panic the man's presence
	in the world like his love is revealed as
	conditional he has refused
	to marry the child's mother
	and every month the mother sends her daughter
	to the man's apartment to ask for
	grocery money they fear
	the father's moods and they fear
	for their well-being
	now this the source of a child's love and
	food has disappeared into the sea fi-
	nally the man erupts out of the ocean
	at her feet a laughing Proteus with water
	streaming from his hair and shoulders the
	child bursts into tears she sobs her
	relationship with the man is fixed in that instant
	on the tectonics of vulnerability and worship
	... a posture of excessive love and enthusiasm
	will characterize her approach to him for
	the man will not yield the power
	that comes from withholding sustenance but
	even as deprivation of food deforms the body
	so too a want of love shapes the human heart
	the girl grows into a woman
	who is reluctant to eat she dedicates her life
	to succoring the vulnerable maimed and

injured animals her woman's heart
weeps for these innocents she
keeps the small dried body of a seahorse
cotton-cushioned in a matchbox on her
bedside table it is from
the beach where her father rose out of the sea it
is a symbol of deep seas within her
—during the time these events occur
Rabbi Tzvi Freeman writes in Canada that the
world lies deep in a dream where anything
is possible but nothing seems to have a goal where
only chaos reigns it takes only to open our ears our
minds and hearts and the objects of this world
fall into place and work together as a single whole
synchronized as they were meant to be
...a century before this event
and these words a poet in Ireland
thinks about loss he writes: —"Margaret
are you grieving over goldengrove unleaving?...now no-
matter child the name sorrows springs are the same" he
writes—"it is the blight man was born for it is Margaret
you mourn for"
millennia
before this in Greece Homer asks: —Αρχη' των κακο'ν
πραγμα'των? —"What
are the long-buried origins of disaster?"

The Owl

A man knocks on a door a
   woman opens it and
   her dog a big
   spotted Boxer leaps up
   "Don't move"
   she says from behind the dog
   "Let him get to know you" the dog
   drags his wet tongue over the man's arms and
   later she tells him
   the spirit of her husband resides
   in the owl that perches outside
   her bedroom window at night "Let's
   make love" she says later but
   the man
   looks out the window in search of the owl

The Woman from the War

Currents move on a river they
carry a woman who navigates their flow
she does not look back as she paddles
away from a man who sleeps in a tent
currents move in the mind of the woman
their movements never rest they move
in a circle
inside the circle is a war
inside the war is another tent
inside the tent is the woman
there are men in the tent they
lie on cots bandaged and bleeding
they moan they cry they die they
are carried into the tent on stretchers
and the woman moves to each of them quickly
she plugs the holes in their bodies she
sews them up she clips their arteries she
wraps them in white cloth
her hands are red with her work
outside that tent and the time of the tent
outside the war and its circle and the flowing
of her mind outside her head outside
the tent with the sleeping man behind her
a woman is on a river her singing is high
and clear the phosphorus
in her bones is on fire
birds cry out from her throat

The Painter's Grandson

~ for Jack Bowman, Carmel, California 1978

Every morning the old man takes
the boy by the hand and waters the flowers takes
a dozen trips with the watering can and the boy
never tires of it the
water rushes out of the long spout and the boy laughs
as it soaks the leaves and
he never lets go of the old man's hand sometimes
the sun lights them up as they walk back and forth
from the gallery
to the flower box on Dolores street and
the courtyard is bright as they move through the light sometimes
it is foggy in Carmel and the courtyard is hushed
with the glow of the fog and then
the man talks to the boy in whispers
and the boy murmurs back in the hushed landscape

A Cold Layer of Fog

Where a cold layer of fog hangs over the land
    a woman sings to herself
    her husband listens he
    hears the words to Jesus Christ, Superstar
    —*That song,* he thinks making love
    while it played on the stereo how many nights?
    over the course of a year it
    is the only memory of his time
    studying Marx and Existentialist Humanism
    Eric Fromm and C. Wright Mills and
    a ballerina now of course
    it is too clichéd to admit but
    then... so new new enough
    to seem . . . epiphanic that much
    he remembers *It always seems so*
    to the young he thinks —*Joyce's*
    quiditatis but now
    the man feels the triteness of memory
    of youth that ballerina
    six foot beautiful taller than im
    blond everywhere! what
    a thing to remember! he shudders
    humiliated at his own callow youth but
    the intensity of the memory alarms him
    at the time it seemed so real so
    immediate so important now
    he wonders how it could have happened at all
    to him who was he? it's
    incomprehensible another life
    which of course it was but

more than that: another dimension
and tonight . . . his wife sings
the lyrics to a song she is too young
to have experienced and he feels
—if not exactly caught out—
surprised by himself was it him at all?
he is looking at something
that throws back more than one image:
a past of acts of possibilities and
all of them serendipitous not of his own making
he does not understand the motives
of that young man
In the Rubaiyat, the poet asks: "Who is the potter, pray
and who the pot?" these words formed
on the lips of a clay vessel and
here now a man thinks —who indeed?
is there hope for the man?
whose pot is he? certainly not his own
if he has learned anything in his life
it is that he is neither the maker
nor the thing of his own making he
is an artifact of other hands and
what he knows of himself if anything
seems very little
what does the man know? only
that the lines his wife sings tonight
take him back to a summer's heat
and nights when he was twenty-three and in love
when the song and the singer were new
and this present knowledge —that
as grateful as he is to have lived those moments–
the awareness of the hearts he broke

now breaks his own he
wonders —if not for the poets could he carry on?
"It is the blight man was born for . . . It
is Margaret you mourn for"
another poet that sort of thing the
soporific song of love has lost its power
to turn the man's mind blank and that
is his melodie au crepuscule
the years' inoculation against both passion
and oblivion
to call his diminished state of being
'wisdom' is another betrayal: no.
some unlovely thing courted by incapacity
has moved into his temple and
thrown out the mystic

The Picture

He returns home early from
    work and quietly enters the house mur-
    mured voices
    reach him from the bedroom he
    pads shoeless over the carpet and
    looks into the room his wife sits
    astride a naked man on the bed "Brook came
    by for a massage" she says the
    man nods silently she
    wears an open terrycloth robe the
    color of a robin's egg nothinng
    beneath it her
    yellow hair falls loosely down her back as
    she re-
    mains astride her client who
    doesn't move who
    stares at the ceiling his arms outstretched
    the palms of his hands upturned
    like Christ on a bed with a peach-colored summer
    quilt the sun streams through the window
    filtered by lace curtains it
    falls upon them it
    fills the room with the bed's blush he
    leaves the scene but the picture
    ––painted with the brush-
    strokes of betrayal and fixed with these colors––
    hangs in his mind

On the Steps of Holy Cross Church

He finds a record of events
forgotten after thirty winters in a drawer
(*how had he lost the note*
describing one incident and two dreams?)
written (as it was) to remind himself
of who he was as
1) he paused upon
the threshold of a church filled with light
and song
looking through the doors that night
was like the vision in a dream
wherein the dreamer stands in shadow
with bright commemorations just a step away
he had moved through dark and time but
light and the moment revealed that
2) once in sleep he traveled through a green land
to a village and a house wherein stretched rows
of mighty gates that guarded rooms filled
with philosophies and knowing
only one among them breathed song
shone red and gold with sunlight and voices that
called to him it was a holy place
filled with the geometries
of his most secret heart and
3) on another night the visions came again
reminding him they were neither of them dreams
but realities
Borges writes in Argentina that archetypes
unrevealed to us perhaps are eternal objects

that gradually enter the world
just as the palace of Kubla Khan uncompleted and in ruins
reappeared centuries later in the dream of an English poet
transcribed upon his waking in a poem
only partially rebuilt by ink and paper —a fragment
whose lines are arguably

the most lyrical in the English language.[1]
In 1797 that poet asks
"If a man could pass through Paradise in a dream
and have a flower given to him as a pledge
that his soul had really been there and
if he found that flower in his hand
when he awoke—Ay!—and what then?"
Upstream in time an unlettered herdsman
is dreaming in a stable
someone on the other side of waking
calls his name commanding him to sing
about the origin of created things the herdsman
recites verses he has never known before
and when he wakes remembers them they
become Caedmon's Hymn perhaps at that point
the most lyrical innovation in Saxon poetry
years later, the herdsman predicts the hour of his death
and waits for it peacefully in sleep
because of such things the Argentine
suggests that *Music* *"states of happiness mythology*
faces molded by time certain twilights and certain places
—all these are trying to tell us something
or have told us something we should not have missed

or are about to tell us something..."[2]

The Dancer

~ for Frieda Sherman, Santa Cruz
    Being eighty and loving with
the fugitive articulation of
limbs in darkness she hears
the hillside horses on the other slope
says "It's time the sun came out"
she pirouettes this side of hope (no longer
nimble as gazelles in sunlight) and
plucks these moments from the fading crys-
talized coherencies with violins on beaches she
dances before the flowing on of flutes

Poem Version

As he stands before the toilet bowl a man
    thinks of his mother it
    occurs to him that she trained him
    to perfect his aim as a toddler
    by an invention "Aim
    into the middle of the water and
    see how many bubbles you can make" she said
    "The more you make . . .
    the more money you'll have when you grow up" it
    hasn't worked out that way but
    even now he is aiming for the middle of the bowl
    and measuring the bubbles hoping
    for money money that remains elusive and
    it occurs to him that his mother's reasoning
    was to limit the mess little boys make
    by aiming poorly a mess that mothers
    had to clean up and wives once
    the boys grew into men with poor aims he's
    heard complaints about such things
    and . . . admittedly he's
    felt disdain at the mess
    on the floors of other bathrooms but
    then (quite suddenly)
    he feels a rush of gratitude toward his mother
    of tenderness and his eyes burn as he stands
    in this absurd and human moment
    while the whole panoply
    of his mother's directives — her patience
    her voice the humor in her voice her
    love and her motives her

tricks and her humanity — envelop him
and he weeps like a child for the past for
the mind of a mother that lives in his own

Children Stories

~ for Frieda

A woman is a dancer she
has six toes she writes fables
and children's stories she keeps a journal she
chronicles the difficulties of marriage writes
of betrayals and forgiveness of
adultery and its lamentations of
being together and growing apart
when her husband dies the dancer shows her journal
and her letters to her friend who is a writer he
reads them and reads the dancer's heart
she asks him if they should be preserved
parts of them published there are poems
in the journal that are very beautiful
they show the dancing of her woman's heart but
her children send her to a nursing home
they take her journals they
do not send them to the man despite
instructions from their mother
the children are shocked by the woman
revealed within the letters she has passion she loves
she hates she rages the children
decide the writings are too personal
for an outsider to see but
the man has already read them and more he
knows the children will remain children
and never see the woman in their mother
but he has seen her has seen
her storms her love and she lives in his mind
in a room that is bright with skylights and glass

she is quiet there and looks out
into the shadowed redwoods of Glenn Canyon Road

When Foxes Dance

~ for Steve Fox

In Santa Cruz the rains blow in with winter
they move in from the sea first
the high cirrus appear
brushing their faint haze around the sun
then the big clouds spun low
and heavy with rain come in
sometimes
a cloud drops its burden
and the rain falls on the town and
the sun pours down through the rain . . . in
Amsterdam they say the devil parties at such
times they call it the Devil's Carnival but
in the Japanese tradition this is the time
when foxes dance yes when
the rains fall through sunshine
the foxes dance and are married
that is the story and because Fox
is the name of the friend he lost a man
keeps that thought in his mind the autumn skies
are clear as he drives out of
Santa Cruz and he looks towards the mountains
where the sun moves sharply through madrone
groves and the rich red bark of the trees peels away
from the smooth skin beneath tight
and curling limbs twisting
in the light dancing &
singing in their brightness

The Woman With Mad Eyes

~ Café Pergolisi, Santa Cruz

A woman with the unutterable eyes of birds
rummages in the café trash for food a
hostage to mistakes she
knows the spider in the corner hears
the braying of wild asses in the crowd she
sees the wolf writing by the door disguised and
sipping coffee

The Psychic in India Joze Café

Santa Cruz

A psychic in a café
sits at a table watching her re-
flection in the window she
preens she poses her face
is spectral in the silvered glass
she has returned from India
and Sai Baba where she ate the ash
from his temple she
gives little samples to the members
in her Church
of the Holy Grail some
trace dark circles on their foreheads others
touch the ash lightly to the tips
of their tongues their actions
are hushed and holy
the Argentinian writes that
"Such symbols are capable of many
perhaps incompatible values
that can be offensive to reason but not
to dreams which have their singular

and secret algebra[1] *"*
and in this ambiguous realm
wherein *"one thing may be many"*
a table in Santa Cruz is graced
with a yellow daffodil a woman
studies her image darkly
in the window-glass

The Sugar Plum Fairy

~ for Ralph

In a flower shop named the Bodacious Begonia
a woman talks in a clear high voice
tracing the intricacies of a budding relationship her
mind skips over the subject
deftly a friend listens from across a table
(privately he calls her the Sugar Plum Fairy) at
the far end of the table a terra cotta pot supports a tangle
of lobelia and violas *the deep purples are
as delicate and as lovely as the petals of the
Sugar Plum's mind* are the thoughts in the mind
of the man a mind that wanders now when
he closes his eyes at night just before sleep
detailed and intricate scenes of foliage speed
past his vision green verdant ferny
close to the ground *such a man
has no idea how to explain it* some-
times perfect and intricate in its detail he thinks
it to be recognizably non-earthly yet
familiar it
alarms him because it makes no sense
the detail is flawless and he knows
which plants do and do not grow on earth yet
it is all familiar and comforting a
sort of secret life glimpsed at the interface of sleep
and waking *perhaps (he thinks) be-
tween the states of being* he
never questions the sanity of it
it makes him happy
he is brought out of his reverie by the sound

of the Sugar Plum's voice she
nibbles away at her subject explaining
her attempts to bring light into the spiritual
penumbra around her he rolls the word around
on his tongue silently like a lozenge pen-umm-bra
"Why" she asks "do so many people
try to convince us we are less than we are?" the
man knows she plays a secret and sporadic pi-
ano how well he cannot know since she allows
no one to hear it with her paintings
she is more generous...

The Cook

~ for Cheryl Millet 1947 — 2019

A moment opens for the woman she
summons cherished thoughts
of home a
room with printed ducks upon a papered
wall— the Abitibi River ribboned with the broken stars —beyond the shoreline's sink of darkness...the forest's summer
peat and in the winter frost patterned
on the window glass up-
on the other side of warmth the night's
alight with snow —an owl's calling home her name
and then . . .again . . .the shape
that visited her windowpane
. . . she wishes to be there but
up from memory she looks across
the kitchen's clatter where her cooks
are toiling at their flames the air hangs heavy
with the present's spice and cumin
in the food— but
What is truth she thinks talking
recently—just yesterday in fact—
someone murmured their good-byes and
said "Enjoy the Dream" like that
with capitals . . .who
says such things. . . more
& more the edges blur between her nights
and days the lines between realities become less desperate
—De Quincey writes:
"Each item in the world's a secret glass or secret

mirror of the universe..." these are the words
her brother spoke be-
fore all this became her life but in
a country colored by the moon
where underneath their snowy shroud a thousand
tiny dreams of fears and greeds stir fitfully within
the furry bodies waiting to awake winter owls un-
moving in the branches watch over
her and at her window frame
a silver horse appears it
rears its head then
spreads its wings and soars
into the night with her. . .

On Both Sides of Dreaming

~ Marc

We look into the dark of night into
the past & finally
into the selves we do not want to see
. . . time ticks
greenly on a bedside
clock like paint upon the watches
of our youth where each small hand
crowned with drops of radium traced
diasporas of time yes
half-lives tick silently
into bloodstreams into
cells and chromosomes of a million children
as absent as our own the pillow's
flat we feel it the air is still
the
movement in our minds is anything but smooth its
ticking persistent im-
placable
above us the smoke detectors
blink —all systems go— life
in a white heat and
the memory of our loves silent and glowing
as we look beyond the green splash of regret
over the door out
through the windows of our grief where
bright and singing Venus
floats upon the solar winds

The Veteran

What
    does the man do when those around him
    are being cut down will he
    ask if he is real is that
    the question —what does the event mean?
    he stands not moving not
    believing until he is pulled down
    by someone behind him *get down*
    get down is he alive
    or is this the last moment
    of consciousness the dream
    of a stretched and final heartbeat how
    long could such a heartbeat last?
    for the man forever to
    the man recurs the old question *Do I wake*
    or sleep is the life I will live real is
    there a difference? one poet writes
    "The moment of the rose and the moment
    of the yew tree are of equal duration" another
    that he dreamed he was talking with a friend who
    "In the world of waking reality
    died many years ago"

The Veteran's Wife

She knows her husband's hollowed
    by his dreams that time
    and moments are a grammar
    that she can not crack he can not say
    the jungles of his dreams
    are sweet though
    northern woods grow resinous with day at
    night he wanders paths
    through small secluded shadows
    in his brain
    the woman
    knows a certainty whose name she dare not
    speak that truths are calls to consequence
    she understands
    to see is to be seen and so her head
    is buried in this morning's pillow as she
    sleeps beside her sleepless husband
    in their bed

A Company of Men

One month after his father died
    and at the same hour
    a man is claimed by a dream he
    walks down a long hall to a room
    where he is expected to give a talk ap-
    proaching the door he sees within
    a round table seated at it
    is a group of his father's friends
    they are gathered to hear an anecdote
    the man is about to recount and his father
    is waiting with them sitting to the right
    of an empty chair reserved for his son a
    little pale and weak and a little
    confused he is there
    to hear a story his son is about to tell it
    is a story of his life he
    has not heard it before and he does not
    know it though the story is his own
    he is interested now and
    wants to hear it told ––to learn it––
    for while he was living he was inside his
    life and could not see his story in its en-
    tirety and so it seems to the son
    not at all strange that the tale
    has not been for his father
    to tell nor
    does it seem odd that it is up
    to a son to begin it in a way
    a father can understand
    among the company of men he has lived with

and loved
only here
can he see what it is for the first time
And so it is for all the men in the room
only the plurality can explain
the singular if it is to be understood
and the story of one man's life is never his own
to recount a life
is a tale that takes many tongues
in the telling so
the younger man leans forward and
puts his hand on the back
of his father's neck and
knows that his father is hurting though
he does not know how he knows
and his father nods softly
the circle of men draw close shoulder
to shoulder and lean forward to hear they
are eager to listen and are happy
to be a part of the story glad
to know that each is giving the sharing
of their lives as a great gift
one to the other they
are grateful that his father
has shared his life with them
and the son is thankful
as he leans forward among them

   "I know a man" he says ...

A Painter

~ for Ralph

She makes gifts of tiny watercolors
to her friends the postcard-sized revelations the
pastel glimpses into her mind un-
spoiled and Jungian she's
shy about them and
he's uneasy when he looks as though
he has unexpectedly come upon her un-
clothed later that day he
tells this to a man he loves
"It's an embarrassing view of her private self"
he says but the Friend answers "No-
one is embarrassed but you" says "Perhaps
when you look into her paintings you
do not see a picture but a mirror..."

You Said

~ for Richard Burrows, London, 1971
    ("...a pair of early morning leopards
    young and sexless..." ~ r. burrows)
      You said "People think they know you they want
      to own it the cheap complacency" and
      I have carried you through life like
      a locket over my most secret heart
      you said *it was the rain you felt*
      when I blew through your mind and
      lay in small pools on the doorsteps
      *of your eye*s you
      knew the places I would not speak of
      the reckless winds the ocean
      shaping the shore
      I watched your eyes
      unsepulcher the rites of spring
      . . . I do not profess to understand it

The Dancer & Henry Miller

The dancer is young she
lives in a house on Pfeiffer Beach seasoned
by years and the sea and her tears
the walls are muralled with brush strokes big and bold yes
life is large on Big Sur and the dancer
telephones the man in the moment
"Come to the beach" she says "We can walk
on the sand and be silly" the man drives from Santa Cruz
to walk by the waves with the dancer her
parties spread to the sea there is laughter
and joy down the road the hot springs
of Esalen offer views of the ocean the baths
are free to locals after midnight "Let's
go have a soak" she says and he drives to her
Nepenthe is just down the road and
the dancer takes lunch there sometimes
she sees Henry Miller eating across the room she
takes the story back to the house on the beach
and says to the man "Henry Miller
lives a five-minute walk down the road
and high on a hill past Nepenthe he's attended
by young women who play ping-pong on his patio they
are nude" she says
Henry Miller sits with his ghosts and watches he
watches the women and watches his guests as they watch
then he writes what he sees...
the man in the moment returns
over the bridge of the years to a time
when the house on the beach is gone and the dancer

no longer dances but she sways in a music
that moves to the pasts that are in her it is
nearly the present in Santa Cruz and
she calls "Come to the beach" she says
to her friend but the beach is long ago and
she lives in the redwoods of Glenn Canyon Road
she calls "Come visit We can do
something silly and walk by the sea"
now
the sea and its tides have become a horizon
and outside the memory and inside the present
the dancer is gone only the moments remain
in the mind of the man
who looks out over Monterey Bay

Winter

Sometimes a shadow
    moves along the night it
    glides through icy slaps it
    snakes through trees above ten-
    thousand teeth asleep
    beneath the snows that bite a thousand
    dreams some-
    times a figure eating oranges by a fire will
    watch the rinds explode like rainbows in the flames
    will sit beside a window ledge
    where frost leaves lace upon the panes while
    outside snow falls cleanly and in banks more
    hushed than wings of owls
    before the burst of talons on the snow that
    marks some termination of a trail ––a signature
    where (see!) a shallow crater blurs
    its quiet edge

<<< . >>>

www.ingramcontent.com/pod-product-compliance
Lightning Source LLC
Chambersburg PA
CBHW021804150726

47989CB00004B/1791